CATS SET VI

AMERICAN WIREHAIR CATS

Jill C. Wheeler
ABDO Publishing Company

Published by ABDO Publishing Company, PO Box 398166, Minneapolis, MN 55439.
Copyright © 2012 by Abdo Consulting Group, Inc. International copyrights reserved
in all countries. No part of this book may be reproduced in any form without written
permission from the publisher. The Checkerboard Library™ is a trademark and logo of
ABDO Publishing Company.

Printed in the United States of America, North Mankato, Minnesota.
102011
012012

 PRINTED ON RECYCLED PAPER

Cover Photo: Photo by Helmi Flick
Interior Photos: Animal Photography pp. 9, 17, 20; Animals Animals p. 19;
    Glow Images p. 15; Photos by Helmi Flick pp. 5, 6, 11, 12

Editors: Tamara L. Britton, BreAnn Rumsch
Art Direction: Neil Klinepier

Library of Congress Cataloging-in-Publication Data

Wheeler, Jill C., 1964-
  American wirehair cats / Jill C. Wheeler.
      p. cm. -- (Cats)
  Includes index.
  ISBN 978-1-61783-238-3
  1. American wirehair cat--Juvenile literature. I. Title.
  SF449.A47W43 2012
  636.822--dc23
                              2011026461

CONTENTS

Lions, Tigers, and Cats 4

American Wirehair Cats 6

Qualities 8

Coat and Color 10

Size 12

Care 14

Feeding 16

Kittens 18

Buying a Kitten 20

Glossary 22

Web Sites 23

Index 24

LIONS, TIGERS, AND CATS

Is your home like one out of every three in the United States? It is if you have at least one cat! There are more than 93 million pet cats in the United States. Among the 42 **domestic** cat **breeds**, looks and personalities vary widely.

Yet even the gentlest house cat has things in common with the fiercest lion. Both cat species belong the biological family **Felidae**. The 37 members of this family are known as felids.

These skilled hunters have sharp claws and teeth. They are graceful and flexible animals, with sharp eyesight and strong muscles. About 3,500 years ago, humans began putting these hunters to use. Ancient Egyptians **domesticated** wildcats. The cats killed the rats and mice that threatened grain stores.

Today, cats come from all over the world. Yet just three **breeds** developed in the United States. One of them is the **unique** American wirehair.

Some cat enthusiasts call American wirehair cats "kinkies."

AMERICAN WIREHAIR CATS

The American wirehair cat is an American original. In 1966, a **litter** of kittens was born at Council Rock Farm in Verona, New York. Several had unusual wiry coats. Unfortunately, a weasel attacked the kittens. Only one survived.

Local **breeder** Joan O'Shea heard about the strange **litter**. O'Shea visited the farm and bought the surviving kitten. She named the red and white **tabby** male Adam. O'Shea bred Adam, which produced more kittens with wiry coats. One named Amy later gave birth to additional wiry-coated kittens.

Scientists eventually determined that the strange coat was caused by a natural genetic mutation. They also learned that the mutation was incomplete. This meant that not every kitten in a litter would have wiry hair. Some might have only a little. Others may have hair that loses its crimp with age.

In 1967, the unusual American wirehair was first recognized by the **Cat Fanciers' Association (CFA)**. Today, breeders are still working to find the best way to produce kittens with wiry coats.

The American wirehair was granted CFA championship status in 1978. Today, the breed is also accepted by the International Cat Association.

QUALITIES

American wirehair owners claim their cats have the best personalities. These cats have a soft voice, which they do not use often. They love to play but are not too active. Some owners have described their wirehairs as being like clowns.

If American wirehairs feel like playing, they may bring a toy to one of their humans as a hint. If they have no toy, they will create one from whatever they can find!

The easygoing wirehair usually gets along with all family members and pets. This makes these cats good additions to the family. However, wirehairs do not need another cat, dog, or human to play with them. So, they also do well in one-owner households.

This **breed** is a good choice for owners who do not want lap cats. Many wirehairs like to be around their owners but not necessarily on them. They are content with lingering nearby rather than on a lap or couch. Some wirehairs may follow their people from room to room.

American wirehair cats are affectionate but do not demand attention. They are sweet and loving without being too clingy.

COAT AND COLOR

The American wirehair's coat is somewhat similar to the American shorthair's. Both are thick and **dense**, and both **shed** moderately.

The one important difference between the two coats is quite obvious! American shorthair cats have short, straight hair while American wirehair cats have coarse, crimped hair. Even their whiskers and the hair inside their ears is crimped, hooked, or bent. If it is long, the wiry hair can form ringlets.

There are more than 27 possible color and pattern variations for this **breed**'s kinky coat. Colors include white, blue, cream, red, silver, brown, and **tortoiseshell**. The coat's pattern can be solid, **bicolored**, **calico**, smoke, **chinchilla**, or **tabby**.

According to **CFA** standards, all American wirehairs must have gold eyes. Silver cats are the exception. They can have blue eyes. Some cats may even have eyes of different colors! **Breeders** call these cats "odd-eyed."

An American wirehair's coat feels springy and wiry to the touch.

SIZE

American wirehair cats are medium to large cats. They have well-developed muscles, which give them a rounded, thick appearance.

These cats are heavier than they look. Strong, medium-sized legs support their body weight. Males grow to weigh an average of 11 to 15 pounds (5 to 7 kg). Adult females are slightly smaller. They average 8 to 12 pounds (3.5 to 5.5 kg).

Thanks to their ancestors and natural build, American wirehairs are natural athletes.

The **breed**'s head has bold cheekbones, a strong jaw, and a well-developed **muzzle** and chin. Its medium-sized ears have rounded tips. Its eyes are large, round, and widely spaced.

Early American wirehairs looked very different from today's wirehair cats. Adam and his **offspring** were tall with long legs. They had long tails, large ears, and almond-shaped eyes. Every single hair on them was crimped. Due to this crimping, it was often possible to see skin through their fur.

As breeders continued to develop the cats, American wirehairs were bred with American shorthairs. This genetic diversity helped to produce healthy animals. Yet, it also had a lasting influence on the look of the wirehair breed.

CARE

It probably comes as no surprise that the American wirehair's coat requires special care. Owners should brush their American wirehairs gently because the curly hair is very fragile. The wiry coat also tends to be oily. So, the cats should be bathed regularly.

American wirehairs can develop skin problems such as allergies. Regular bathing can help with this. Owners also should check for waxy buildup in the wirehair's ears. Problems can arise if the buildup is not removed regularly.

These cats do not get sick often. However, it is still important to visit the veterinarian. He or she will provide yearly checkups and **vaccines**. The veterinarian can also **spay** or **neuter** these cats.

Owners should provide their wirehair with things it needs to be comfortable indoors. Toys will keep it mentally and physically busy. A scratching post will allow the cat to sharpen its claws without destroying furniture. And, a **litter box** will allow the cat to bury its waste as it would in nature.

An indoor lifestyle is safest for a pet cat. It can also add to your pet's life span.

FEEDING

Felids are carnivores, and American wirehair cats are no exception. Like all **domestic** cats, they should eat high-quality cat food that has plenty of protein.

Owners may choose from dry, moist, and semimoist foods. Make sure the food label says "balanced" and "complete." Fresh water should also be supplied every day.

Because of their crimped hair, American wirehairs can easily form hair balls. These are bits of swallowed hair or fur that form into clumps in the cat's stomach. **Breeders** recommend that owners use a hair ball preventative. One solution is providing food high in vegetable fiber.

Just like people, cats enjoy an occasional treat. But be careful! American wirehairs can become overweight. Leaving out large amounts of food all day encourages overeating. So, one way to protect against overeating is to feed the cat one meal at a time.

If you are concerned about your cat's weight, check with your veterinarian.

KITTENS

American wirehair cats make excellent parents. Females can begin having **litters** around seven to nine months of age. After mating, they are **pregnant** for about 65 days. Litters average four to six kittens.

The kittens are blind and deaf at birth. They depend on their mother for food and protection. After about three weeks, kittens have developed functioning senses. When they are five weeks old, kittens can start to eat regular cat food.

Still, it is best to keep kittens with their mothers until they are about 12 to 16 weeks old. By then, a good **breeder** will have given the kittens their first **vaccines**. The kittens will also know how to use a **litter box** by this age.

Your American wirehair kitten may have a favorite person, but don't worry! It will still make time for all family members.

Unlike some other **breeds**, an American wirehair kitten will become attached to all members of its human family. With proper care, this special feline family member can live for 7 to 12 years.

Buying a Kitten

Due to the challenges of **breeding** cats with a natural genetic mutation, American wirehairs are rare. Show-quality wirehairs are especially rare.

In the first 21 years wirehairs were recognized by the CFA, just 425 cats were registered. This number continues to grow slowly.

So, families who want a pet American wirehair likely will get a "straight wire" kitten. These cats lack the wirehair gene and cannot compete at cat shows. With ordinary coats, these cats may not look as **unique**. But, they still possess the wirehair's sweet, loving personality.

Families who want to adopt an American wirehair should first find a reputable **breeder**. There will likely be a waiting list. Those wishing to purchase an American wirehair kitten must also be willing to pay for one. Purebred cats can range from several hundred to several thousand dollars.

Once you have chosen a kitten, check it for signs of good health. Its ears, nose, mouth, and fur should be clean. The eyes should be bright and clear. Then, all there will be left to do is to take your kitten home!

When you do, be prepared to answer questions about your new pet. People will probably ask, "What kind of kitten is *that*?"

GLOSSARY

bicolored - having two colors.

breed - a group of animals sharing the same ancestors and appearance. A breeder is a person who raises animals. Raising animals is often called breeding them.

calico - a coat pattern featuring white fur with patches of two other colors, most commonly black and red.

Cat Fanciers' Association (CFA) - a group that sets the standards for judging all breeds of cats.

chinchilla - a shaded coat pattern featuring color only on the tips of the hairs.

dense - thick or compact.

domestic - tame, especially relating to animals. To domesticate something is to adapt it to life with humans.

Felidae (FEHL-uh-dee) - the scientific Latin name for the cat family. Members of this family are called felids. They include lions, tigers, leopards, jaguars, cougars, wildcats, lynx, cheetahs, and domestic cats.

litter - all of the kittens born at one time to a mother cat.

litter box - a box filled with cat litter, which is similar to sand. Cats use litter boxes to bury their waste.

muzzle - an animal's nose and jaws.

neuter (NOO-tuhr) - to remove a male animal's reproductive glands.

offspring - the young of a plant or an animal.

pregnant - having one or more babies growing within the body.

shed - to cast off hair, feathers, skin, or other coverings or parts by a natural process.

spay - to remove a female animal's reproductive organs.

tabby - a coat pattern featuring stripes or splotches of a dark color on a lighter background. Individual hairs are banded with light and dark colors.

tortoiseshell - a coat pattern featuring patches of black, orange, and cream.

unique - being the only one of its kind.

vaccine (vak-SEEN) - a shot given to prevent illness or disease.

WEB SITES

To learn more about American wirehair cats, visit ABDO Publishing Company online. Web sites about American wirehair cats are featured on our Book Links page. These links are routinely monitored and updated to provide the most current information available.

www.abdopublishing.com

INDEX

A
adoption 18, 21

B
body 12
breeder 7, 11, 13, 16,
    18, 21

C
care 14, 15, 16, 17, 19
Cat Fanciers'
    Association 7, 11
character 8, 9, 18, 21
claws 15
coat 6, 7, 10, 11, 14,
    16, 21
color 7, 10, 11

E
ears 10, 13, 14, 21
eyes 11, 13, 21

F
Felidae (family) 4
food 16, 17, 18

G
grooming 14

H
head 13
health 13, 14, 16, 17, 21
history 4, 5, 6, 7, 13

K
kittens 6, 7, 18, 19, 21

L
legs 12
life span 19
litter box 15, 18

M
muzzle 13, 21

N
neuter 14
nose 21

O
O'Shea, Joan 7

R
reproduction 7, 18

S
scratching post 15
senses 18
shedding 10
size 12, 13
skin 14
spay 14

T
toys 8, 15
training 18

U
United States 4, 5,
    6, 7

V
vaccines 14, 18
veterinarian 14
voice 8

W
water 16
weight gain 17
whiskers 10